Rock
Collectors

Herbert Brunkhorst
&
Bonnie Brunkhorst

Dominie Press, Inc.

Publisher: Christine Yuen
Series Editors: Adria F. Klein & Alan Trussell-Cullen
Editors: Bob Rowland & Paige Sanderson
Photographer: Y. Raymond
Designers: Gary Hamada, Lois Stanfield, & Vincent Mao

Photo Credits: Graham Meadows (Page 8-inset)

Published by:

⚡ Dominie Press, Inc.

1949 Kellogg Avenue
Carlsbad, California 92008 USA

www.dominie.com

ISBN 0-7685-0569-0

Printed in Singapore

14 15 16 17 18 V0ZF 15 14 13

Table of Contents

"Rocks are ugly," said Rajah.

"No, they're not," said Kaira.
"Rocks are interesting.
Rocks can be pretty, too."

"These rocks aren't pretty,"
said Rajah.
"These rocks are dirty."

"You can wash off the dirt,"
said Kaira.
"Now look at the different colors."

"These rocks are hard," said Rajah.

"Hard rocks are useful,"
said Kaira.
"Roads and sidewalks are
made from hard rocks."

"This rock breaks," said Rajah.
"This rock is not useful."

"Yes it is," said Kaira.
"Broken rocks are useful, too.
Broken rocks make sand.
We like to play in the sand."

"I want to start a rock collection," said Kaira.

"I will help you," said Rajah.

"I will help you, too,"
said their mother.

"Look at these rocks," said Kaira.
"I found them today."

Pink and Black roads
Sand roads

14

They picked the best rocks.
They put them in a box.
Their mother helped them
write labels.

"You are right," said Rajah.
"Rocks are interesting!"

Pink and Black rock
Sand rock

18

"And they're useful, too!"
said their mother.

Picture Glossary

labels:

rocks:

rock collection:

sand:

Index